# WARFARE 101

*S. M. Conner*

Unless otherwise indicated, all Scripture quotations are taken from the King James Version of the Bible.

# DEDICATION

This book is dedicated to Yvonne Moore of Kingston, Jamaica and Esther Ilnisky of Lighthouse Christian Center in West Palm Beach Florida. Thank you for mentoring me in intercession, warfare and the prophetic.

# ACKNOWLEDGEMENTS

Our Lord Jesus Christ whose name makes all things possible. My best friend and husband Eben. My beautiful daughter Heaven. Monita Sharpe – thank you for editing over and over again. Lisa Fuller, thanks for asking me a million questions on warfare which forced me to put it on paper! All the members of the Body of Christ who desire to engage in warfare, this simple book is for you.

# FOREWORD

The Body of Christ has been yearning for a deeper spiritual connection with our Creator. Could it be that people feel disconnected, defeated and displaced even though they are a part of the family of God? Could it be that for so long, we have produced an immature and ill-equipped army of God dependent upon the arm of flesh? I am personally convinced that some of the missing links in the lives of many are a lack of understanding of prayer and warfare.

It is time for us to get back to the basics of helping others to understand the importance of a personal relationship with God and provide the tools necessary for them to defeat the enemy in their personal lives. Warfare 101 is one of those tools.

My wife has a diverse background and has been dealing with spiritual warfare matters for most of her life. She is well versed in this subject and offers the new believer a simple approach to warfare while educating other believers on its value in the Christian life. Your life or your ministry will benefit from this awesome work.

*Pastor Eben Conner*
Word of Truth Family Church

# CONTENTS

# INTRODUCTION

*Therefore the business of waging war lies in carefully studying the designs of the enemy.*

Sun Tzu

On several occasions I have been approached regarding the subject of spiritual warfare. Though we are engaged in an unrelenting battle, I have discovered that many Christians are either afraid of warfare or they avoid it as a subject that should be dealt with by five fold ministers. Not many Christians believe that they should be actively involved in spiritual warfare. There is a percentage of believers that accept the responsibility of engaging in spiritual warfare but are limited in their involvement because they have not been taught the principles of warfare. With this in mind, the information in this book is geared toward equipping the saints in the basic art of spiritual warfare.

**2 Corinthians 2:11**
*Lest Satan should get an advantage of us: for we are not ignorant of his devices.*

To win any type of war, there has to be an understanding of war.

We must know why we are fighting, who we are fighting and which army we are enlisted in. Greater details such as information about out commanding officer, our weapons of war, our enemy and his strategies, our rank, position and measure of authority, must be clearly understood and accepted. Let's discover and study what the scriptures reveal about this subject. By no means am I declaring to you that this book entails everything you need to know; I am however promising you that if you have never engaged in spiritual warfare you will learn the basic principles of discerning, disarming and destroying satanic influences in your life.

## WHAT IS WARFARE ANYWAY?

Warfare is armed conflict between enemies. The kingdom of God is in a battle against the kingdom of Satan. The kingdom of darkness strategizes and plots against the kingdom of God and His saints with the sole purpose of destroying the testimony of Jesus Christ and capturing souls.

The Old Testament defines war by using the Hebrew word *tsaba'* which means to wage war, to muster an army, to serve in worship. This verb appears 14 times in biblical Hebrew.

Another word, *Lacham*, means to engage in battle or fight. This verb occurs 171 times in biblical Hebrew. Finally, *milchamah* which means to battle or war occurs more than 300 times in the Old Testament, indicating how large a part military experience and terminology played in the life of the ancient Israelites. This word means "war," the over-all confrontation of two forces (Gen. 14:2). It can refer to the engagement in hostilities considered as a battle (Gen. 14:8) or of the hand-to-hand fighting which takes place.

In Genesis 3:15, God told the serpent that there would be enmity between him and the seed of the woman. The seed of the woman being Christ and the serpent being the Devil. This war has been going on for ages.

God has plans and promises for His children. In order to keep His children from their inheritance in Christ or to hinder others from coming to Him, the enemy engages us in a battle.

# DISCERNING THE ENEMY

*If you do not know what you are fighting, you will never know when you have won.*

A great part of discerning the enemy involves understanding his character. It is the nature of the Devil to kill, steal and destroy (Jn. 10:10). Wherever any of those things are present, one of two things has happened. Either the enemy is at work or we have made poor choices.

We have an archenemy that hates our God and us. He purposely attacks us as believers with the goal that we will forsake God. He understands that away from God, we have no true life. Using deception and strategic planning, satan tries to diminish our concept of God.

If you are currently under a spiritual attack, cheer up - we win. God is not slack concerning His promises. Dust off the remnants of depression and weariness and let's take back what the devil tried to steal.

## HOW DO I KNOW IF I AM UNDER ATTACK?

How do you know when the experiences you are going through are the Devil or your flesh? Basic common sense, personal inventory and discernment can answer that question. Over the years, I have seen people try to give the devil credit for 'making' them sin.

Imagine this, a single woman decides she is bored of being single. She willingly goes to a nightclub and begins to flirt just to make sure she still has what it takes to 'catch a husband'. After a while, she meets a guy who seems to be a great catch. Good looking, nice car hmmmn, even has a job! Imagine that! So, in order to not let this fish get back into the sea of bachelors, she allows him to get physically involved with her and she fornicates.

Clearly, this was her flesh. Yet, so many people say 'The devil should not have built that nightclub', 'Once I started, I just could not stop.' You can stop and if you are going to be able to discern between the devil, your flesh or a test, you will need to eliminate the excuses. The first one being, living an unholy lifestyle.

Secondly, take a personal inventory. Thirdly, understand that God is good and not evil. His intentions toward you are for peace. God may use a terrible situation for your betterment. He is not the direct administrator of evil. He knows about it, but does not do it. Satan, his devils or poor choices that give bad consequences the opportunity to wreak havoc in your life are often the sources to your predicament.

**James 1:17**
*'All good gifts come from God...'*

I believe that anything and everything that is good in my life comes from God. I also understand the judgement of God and the 'Job principle'. The Job principle is when Satan has to obtain permission from God to inflict an attack on you. I find that this permission is sought when the person in question is maintaining their covenant with God.

## THE PERSONAL INVENTORY

In order for me to assess whether a situation is an attack, I do a personal inventory. Have I been consistently tithing? If I am not, I have placed myself under the curse that God declared in Malachi 3:9-10. Am I obedient and submitted to authority? Am I covered as an active member of a local church? Am I praying for those in authority? The Bible says that when I pray for those in authority I will live in peace. If I am living in chaos I check my praying. Am I studying His Word? Am I being obedient to the laws of God that I know?

Then I ask the not so obvious questions. Am I walking in worry and anxiety? In Matthew 6, Christ commands us to not worry. Am I honoring my husband as my godly leader? Am I giving honor to my wife as the weaker vessel so that my prayers will not be hindered? Do I give place to the Devil by indulging in the works of the flesh (Galatians 5:16).

After those questions are answered in the positive and I know that I am doing all I know to do that is when I consider the 'Job principle'. The enemy's intent in the Job principle is that we will curse God and die. At this point we must understand that God is aware of everything that is happening. He is still in control. He knows that we are stronger with Him than we are by ourselves.

Our attitude when we are under this kind of attack should not be one of acceptance. Rather than sitting down and accepting the attack, fight back. Keep your heart and lips pure and give God glory. Giving God praise in the midst of a bad situation shows the enemy he is still losing!

Bear in mind that the devil is an agent that God can use to mature you. Ask yourself the question 'What can I learn out of this? What can I give God out of this? Sometimes these situations are necessary for us to see the intent of our hearts.

Some things that happen to us are not attacks. They are the harvests of disobedience. Galatians state that when we sow of the flesh we shall reap corruption. The book of Proverbs declares that there is a way that seems right unto man but the end thereof is destruction. When we disobey God's commands and ignore His principles we are operating in rebellion. Rebellion is the sin that got Lucifer expelled from Heaven. When we act in rebellion like the devil then he uses that familiar place as a means to harass us and we have willingly opened ourselves to demonic activity. It is illogical to think that we can act like the devil and not live in hell/chaos.

## RECOGNIZING DEMONIC ACTIVITY

The most common demonic activity is easily discerned through:

❖ Chronic and consistent financial problems.

❖ Abnormal psychotic behavior. Such as disappearing for days, behaving out of character.

❖ Mental Illness; hallucinations, multiple personalities etc.

❖ Incomprehensible sickness; illnesses that cannot be physically attributed.

❖ Unusual violence and loss of memory after performing an act of violence.

❖ Inexplicable torment and turmoil in marriage.

❖ Injustice & unfair treatment, especially if you cannot attach the injustice or treatment to a personal action.

❖ Governments, systems, etc. that oppose the work of God.

❖ Dreams that incite fear and leave you drained physically.

❖ Personal consistent persecution and trials.

## DISCERNING THE SEASONS OF ATTACK

Certain events in your life have spiritual significance and meaning. Israel's exodus from Egypt had several implications. It was the birthing of a new season, liberation from slavery, land ownership and the entering of the Israelites into the Promised Land. No wonder they received so much persecution and were chased through the Red Sea! Some events attract attack. Here are a few:

❀ The birth of a child destined to be a great leader for God as in the case of Jesus.

❀ A geographical move. Territorial spirits are assigned to cities, states and countries.

❀ A promotion on your job or in the spirit.

❀ Acquiring real estate in any form.

❀ When you are physically tired or exhausted. Remember the story of David and Bathsheeba.

❀ When a miracle has just left the hand of God for you as in the case of Daniel.

❀ When you increase in revelation about the enemy.

❀ When there is disunity in the home or church.-

# 2

# PRIMARY PRINCIPLES OF WAR

> *"The bravest are surely those who have the clearest vision of what is before them, glory and danger alike, and yet not withstanding go out and meet it."*
>
> *Thucydides*

Every army has basic training. You are told where and when to wear the different types of uniforms. You are told who is in charge, your rank, position and assignment which is to eliminate the enemy.

In order to be effective in spiritual warfare there are three primary principles that must be grasped. They are: knowing who is your commanding officer, what is your position and what is your authority.

## WHO IS GOD?

**Exodus 15:3**
*The LORD is a man of war; the LORD is his name.*

We know Him through His Word. A global mistake Christians make in warfare is, battling without knowledge and wisdom. God's Word is the primary source of knowing about God and His magnificent

POWER. Meditate (muse over, say aloud) on and memorize the following verses. Allow them to penetrate your mind and lodge in your spirit. This exercise builds our confidence in war.

## GOD IS:

**Spirit** — John 4:24
*God is a Spirit: and they that worship him must worship him in spirit and in truth.*

**The Creator of all things** — Genesis 1:1
*In the beginning God created the heaven and the earth.*

**The Father of Christ** — Mark 1:11
*And there came a voice from heaven, saying, Thou art my beloved Son, in whom I am well pleased.*

**Not a man** — Num. 23:19
*God is not a man, that he should lie; neither the son of man, that he should repent: hath he said, and shall he not do it? or hath he spoken, and shall he not make it good?*

**Love** — 1John 4:8
*He that loveth not knoweth not God; for God is love.*

**Our peace** — Eph. 2:14
*For he is our peace, who hath made both one, and hath broken down the middle wall of partition between us.*

In the ancient world a person's name revealed his nature. The Names of God define His character and describe His abilities. It is imperative that we know the different names so we can accurately address Him when we are asking Him to specifically intervene. The name Jehovah is a combination of the original Hebrew name for God - Yahweh (I am who I am) and the vowels of Adonai (my Lord). This occurred in the medieval period because the late Old Testament Jews would not pronounce the sacred name of Yahweh. As a matter of fact, they translated Yahweh into LORD in English translations for the same reason.

**Yahweh** — Exodus 3:14
*I am who I am, I will be who I will be*

**Jehovah - Jireh** — Genesis 22:14
*The LORD Will Provide*

**Jehovah - Shammah** — Ezekiel 48:35
*The LORD Is There*

**Jehovah - Shalom** — Judges 6:24
*The LORD Is Peace*

**Jehovah - Rapha** — Exodus 15:26
*I am the LORD that Heals*

**Jehovah - Tsebaoth** — 1Samuel 1:3
*The LORD of Hosts*

**Jehovah Tsidkenu** — Jeremiah 33:16
*The LORD our Righteousness*

**Elohe Israel** — 1Samuel 15:29
*This is synonymous with **Netsah Israel-
LORD** God of Israel / The Strength of Israel*

**The Almighty** — Genesis 49:25

**Almighty God** — Genesis 17:1

**King of Kings, Lord of Lords** — 1Timothy 6:15

**The Alpha and Omega** — Revelation 1:8

**The Beginning and the End** — Revelation 21:6

**I Am** — Exodus 3:14

**Father** — Matthew 5:16

**El Olam** — Genesis 21:33
*(The Everlasting God)*

**El Shaddai** — Exodus 6:3
*(The Breasted One, God Almighty)*

**El Elyon, Addonai,**

**Elohim** — Genesis 1:1-3

## KNOWING YOUR VALUE TO GOD

Knowing who you are to Him and what you are in Him will assist you in seeing how much authority in Christ you possess. In Christ you are:

> *Justified and Redeemed* — Romans 3:24
> *Being **justified** freely by his grace through the **redemption** which is in Christ Jesus.*

> *Complete* — Colossians 2:10
> *And ye are **complete** in him who is the head of all principality and power.*

> *Accepted* — Ephesians. 1:6
> *To the praise of the glory of his grace, wherein he hath made us **accepted** in the beloved.*

> *Wonderfully made* — Psalm 139:14
> *I will praise thee for I am fearfully and **wonderfully** made.*

**A new creature** — 2Corinthians 5:17
*Therefore if any man be in Christ, he is a **new creature**: old things are passed away and behold all things are become new.*

**Royalty** — 1Peter 2:9
*But ye are a chosen generation, a **royal** priesthood, an holy nation, a peculiar people; that ye should show forth the praises of him who has called you out of darkness into his marvelous light.*

**Forgiven** — Ephesians 1:7
*In whom we have redemption through his blood, the **forgiveness** of sins, according to the riches of his grace.*

**Liberated** — Galatians 5:1
*Stand fast therefore in the **liberty** wherewith Christ hath made us free, and be not entangled again with the yoke of bondage.*

**A Child of God** — Romans 8:16
*The Spirit itself beareth witness with our spirit, that we are the **children of God**.*

**Loved greatly** — Romans 8:39
*Nor height, nor depth, nor any other creature shall be able to separate us from the **love** of God, which is in Christ Jesus our Lord.*

**Safe** — John 10:29
*My father, which gave them me, is greater than all; and no man is able to pluck then out of my Father's hand.*

**Triumphant** — 2Corinthians 2:14
*Now thanks be unto to God, which always causes us to **triumph** in Christ, and maketh manifest the savor of his knowledge by us in every place.*

***His workmanship*** — Ephesians 2:10
*For we are **his workmanship**, created in Christ Jesus unto good works, which God hath before ordained that we should walk in them.*

***Sealed with the Holy Spirit*** — Ephesians 1:13
*In whom ye also trusted, after that ye heard the word of truth, the gospel of your salvation: in whom also, after that ye believed, ye were **sealed** with that Holy Spirit of promise.*

***Provided for*** — 2 Peter 1:3
*According as his divine power hath **given unto us** all things that pertain unto life and godliness, through the knowledge of him that hath called us to glory and virtue.*

***Never alone*** — Joshua 1:5
*There shall not any man be able to stand before thee all the days of thy life: as I was with Moses, so **I will be with thee**: I will not fail thee, nor forsake thee.*

## KNOWING YOUR AUTHORITY IN CHRIST

It is important to know your position. If you are not convinced of the supremacy of Christ in **YOU**, fear and intimidation will overtake you. Those are the ingredients of a lost fight. **MEMORIZE** and **MEDITATE** on the following scriptures. Without the conviction of victory and the assurance of your authority, rank and position in Christ, you are guaranteed to lose every time. You have to accept the position God has given you as a son and heir. The son of God came to the sons of men so that sons of men could become sons of God. Pray from your position as a son and not your condition.

**2 Tim 1:7**
*For God hath not given us the spirit of fear; but of* **power**,
*and of love, and of a sound mind.*

**Mark 6:7**
*And he called unto him the twelve, and began to send
them forth by two and two; and* **gave them power** *over
unclean spirits;*

**Matt 28:18**
*And Jesus came and spake unto them, saying,* **All** *power
is given* **unto me** *in heaven and in earth.*

**Matt 10:1**
*And when he had called unto him his twelve disciples,* **he
gave them power** *against unclean spirits, to cast them
out, and to heal all manner of sickness and all manner
of disease.*

**Luke 4:36**
*And they were all amazed, and spake among themselves,
saying, What a word is this! for* **with authority and
power** *he* **commandeth** *the unclean spirits,* **and they
come out.**

**Luke 9:1**
*Then* **he** *called his twelve disciples together, and* **gave them
power** *and* **authority** *over* **all devils**, *and to* **cure diseases.**

**I John 4:4**
*Ye are of God, little children, and have overcome them:
because* **greater is he that is in you**, *than he that is in
the world.*

**Colossians 2:15**
*And having spoiled principalities and powers,* **he** *made a
shew of them openly,* **triumphing** *over them in it.*

**Luke 10:19**
*Behold, **I give unto you power** to tread on serpents and scorpions, and **over all the power of the enemy**: and nothing shall by any means hurt you.*

**Mark 16:17**
*And these signs shall follow them that believe; **In my name** shall **they** cast out devils; they shall speak with new tongues;*

**James 2:19**
*Thou believest that there is one God; thou doest well: **the devils also believe, and tremble**.*

**Ephesians 6:12**
*For we wrestle not against flesh and blood, but against principalities, against powers, against the rulers of the darkness of this world, against spiritual wickedness in high places.*

**Ephesians 1:20 - 21**
*Which he wrought in Christ, when he raised him from the dead, and set him at his own right hand in the heavenly places, Far above all principality, and power, and might, and dominion, and every name that is named, not only in this world, but also in that which is to come: **You are seated in heavenly places with Christ Jesus***

**Phillippians 2:10**
*That at the name of Jesus **every knee** should bow, of things in heaven, and things in earth, and things under the earth;*

**Romans 14:11**
*For it is written, As I live, saith the Lord, **every knee shall bow to me**, and every tongue shall confess to God.*

# POSITIONS OF WAR

*"Do not depend on the enemy not coming; depend rather on being ready for him. Do not depend on the enemy not attacking; depend rather on having a position that cannt be attacked."*

*Sun Tzu*

There is a certain militant posture that should be held in warfare. If you are engaged in prayers that are directed toward the destruction of the works of the devil some positions should be avoided. Some positions represent retreat and surrender. We are not those who retreat but those who forcefully advance! During warfare, refrain from the following:

**Praying with your head bowed** is indicative of submission and surrender. In warfare, your head should be held straight in confidence and authority.

**Holding hands in a circle** is symbolic of unity. However, you have never seen on the news any militant army fighting their enemies holding hands. It eliminates the use of your arms, which you need in order to deploy your weapons.

**Sitting down** is another posture that should be avoided as it signifies being at ease and at rest. If you are in a war you are active not resting. Sitting down gives the enemy an advantage. When sitting you are not as quick to respond as you would be on your feet.

**The ideal position** should be standing erect, head lifted, arms free and your face having a sober expression. We have an enemy who strategizes against us and for the most part, the Body of Christ is laughing as he destroys their homes, churches and communities.

# DON'T FORGET

- **Hold head erect**

- **Keeps eyes open**

- **Focus**

- **Follow the Leader**

- **Do not hold hands in a circle**

CHAPTER

# 4

# THE DRESS CODE

*Prepare for the battle or perish from the results.*

**Every army has its fatigues.** The army of God is no different. We have certain garments that we are required to wear. Our God has given us an ARMOR to put on. The armor is also part of the weapons that we use in warfare.

### Ephesians 6:11,13
*Put on the whole armour of God, that ye may be able to stand against the wiles of the devil.*

*Wherefore take unto you the whole armour of God, that ye may be able to withstand in the evil day, and having done all, to stand.*

As with everything else in the army, the various parts of the armor have individual significance.

### Ephesians 6:14-18
*Stand therefore, having your **loins** girt about with **truth**, and having on the **breastplate of righteousness**; And your **feet** shod with the preparation of the **gospel of peace**; Above all, taking the **shield of faith**, wherewith ye shall be able to quench all the fiery darts of the wicked. And take the **helmet of** salvation, and the **sword of the Spirit**, which is the word of God: **Praying always** with all prayer and supplication in the Spirit, and **watching** thereunto with all **perseverance** and supplication for all saints;*

# ■ Loins girt about with TRUTH

Truth here is from the Greek word 'alethia' which means fact or verity. We must have a life filled with the truth of God's Word and manifesting integrity in our hearts. Our loins or reproductive organs are covered with truth because out of our bellies shall flow rivers of living waters. If we are covered with falsehood and error, we will reproduce that and greater yet, we will be exemplifying a trait that is common to the kingdom of darkness. You cannot know truth unless you understand and apply the Bible. Your measure of truth is based upon that fact. You cannot defeat the enemy by accepting myths, theories and hypotheses. You defeat him with the Truth of God's Word.

# ■ Breastplate of Righteousness

The breastplate covers the chest and heart area. This is where the issues of life flow from. Intentions and motivations are formulated here. The breastplate is to protect and ensure that these areas stay pure before God. Righteousness means 'the state of being right before God' which is achieved only through salvation (the act of accepting Christ's blood sacrifice and redemptive work on the cross). The Breastplate of Righteousness is covering you if you have made Jesus Christ the Lord of your life.

# ■ Feet shod with the Preparation of the Gospel of Peace

The feet are used to travel. Peace means tranquility – a state of being unruffled, whole and complete. The enemy is the author of confusion and chaos. Wherever you go, if you carry the message of the gospel (good news) of peace it counteracts and defeats the confusion of the enemy.

## ■ Shield of Faith

During the time that the Bible was being written, the soldiers had a shield as a part of their armor. This shield would range from 7-10 feet depending on the height of the soldier. It was designed to completely cover the soldier from the feet to the neck. It was used to block arrows whether they were fiery or not. Notice that our shield is one of faith that comes by the Word of God. Faith is the full assurance or conviction of a thing. Faith is the beginning of everything. We need to understand what faith truly means if we are going to be successful in war. How can you win if you do not have the faith that you will?

**Hebrews 11:1 states:**
*Now faith is the substance of things hoped for,*
*the evidence of things not seen.*

Faith is. It is in the present tense. Faith is the foundation, the beginning of things hoped for, the proof or evidence of things not seen. If faith is the beginning, let's explore what other things were in the beginning.

**John 1:1**
*In the **beginning**, was the **Word** and the Word*
*was with God and the Word was God.*

**Genesis 1:1**
*In the **beginning**, God created the heavens*
*and the earth.*

God created the Heavens and the earth by His WORD (Geneses 1:1-31)

The Bible states in Habbakuk 2:4, that the just shall live by faith. In the New Testament, Jesus declares that man should not live by bread alone but by every WORD that proceeds out of the mouth of God. Therefore, it is safe to conclude that faith is equal to the Word of God. Faith is the FOUNDATION, the BEGINNING – have faith.

## ■ Helmet of Salvation

The helmet is used to protect the head. The head contains the brain – the central organ used to control the functions of the body. It is important to cover our minds because this is where the battle begins. Salvation is from the Greek word *sozo*. It means to be made complete or whole. You cannot be in a war and be unsure or confused about the strategy and intent of the war. Your mind needs to be stable or else the enemy who is a mastermind at mind games will intimidate you to the point of retreat.

## ■ Sword of the Spirit

This is the word of God. This is the only part of the armor that is an **OFFENSIVE WEAPON**. Everything else is protective in nature. That is an indication of how much attack one can come under. Notice also that Satan does not just attack you in one area. If it were so, we would not have needed the armor to cover so many places. The Sword of the Spirit: which is the Word of God destroys the works of the enemy.

**Hebrews 4:12**
*For the word of God is quick, and powerful, and sharper than any twoedged sword, piercing even to the dividing asunder of soul and spirit, and of the joints and marrow, and is a discerner of the thoughts and intents of the heart.*

Therefore it is **CRUCIAL** to **KNOW** the **WORD**. To not know it is to commit **SUICIDE** in war. This is the reason that I included the scriptures earlier. Until I knew and **BELIEVED** the **WORD**, I was not only **TERRIFIED** of the devil – I deliberately did whatever it took to not 'upset' him. Once I meditated on the scriptures, I realized that the devil is under the Lordship of Christ and he must obey Him in me.

## OTHER WEAPONS OF WAR

### 2 Corinthians 10:3-5
*For though we walk in the flesh, we do not war after the flesh: (For the weapons of our warfare are not carnal, but mighty through God to the pulling down of strong holds;) Casting down imaginations, and every high thing that exalteth itself against the knowledge of God, and bringing into captivity every thought to the obedience of Christ;*

We are not fighting a physical or natural battle. We are waging war against the kingdom of darkness. We have to use spiritual weapons and arson in order to destroy our enemy. We do this in the form of declaration. Words are creative and constructive. They manifest whatever is said.

■ **The Name of Jesus:**
Remember to use and enter warfare in Jesus' name. The Name of Jesus the Christ is important because He is the one who conquered death and the grave. He is the one who completed the redemptive work required by God. He is the one that is respected in the spirit world as the all time champion. You cannot enter warfare in your own name. You must be commissioned by another who is higher than you – Jesus.

### 1 Corinthians 9:7
*Who goeth a warfare any time at his own charges? who planteth a vineyard, and eateth not of the fruit thereof? or who feedeth a flock, and eateth not of the milk of the flock?*

If you go in your own authority, you will be overtaken and embarrassed. You will be beaten easily and quickly. Always use the Name of Jesus.

### Acts 19:14
*And there were seven sons of one Sceva, a Jew, and chief of the priests, which did so. And the evil spirit answered and said, Jesus I know, and Paul I know; but who are ye? And the man in whom the evil spirit was leaped on them, and overcame them, and prevailed against them, so that they fled out of that house naked and wounded.*

### Mark 16:17
*And these signs shall follow them that believe; **In my name** shall they cast out devils; they shall speak with new tongues;*

### John 16:23
*And in that day ye shall ask me nothing. Verily, verily, I say unto you, Whatsoever ye shall ask the Father **in my name**, he will give it you.*

The Name of Jesus is used in statements like these:

> 'I command you in the Name of Jesus to release *so and so*'.

> 'Poverty, in Jesus' name release your hold on the people of God'.

## ■ The Blood of Jesus

Declaring this over a person or a situation, reminds the enemy of the eternal victory Jesus accomplished at Calvary. Jesus' blood is unique. It is alive and continuously working redemption. Though the death on the cross is over, Jesus' blood still redeems people everyday from sin. It is important to declare or plead the blood in warfare. Satan's kingdom uses blood sacrifices. They understand the power of the blood covenant and the blood sacrifice. Whenever you apply His blood in a given situation or fight, it causes the enemy to retreat because of its significance.

**Ephesians 1:7**
*In whom we have redemption through his blood, the forgiveness of sins, according to the riches of his grace;*

**Colossians 1:20**
*And, having made peace through the blood of his cross, by him to reconcile all things unto himself; by him, I say, whether they be things in earth, or things in heaven.*

Declaring or pleading the Blood is made in statements such as these:

> 'I plead the blood of Jesus over my mind and body.'

> 'The blood of Jesus the Christ is against you,'

## ■ Praise & Worship

This weapon of war is very powerful. Anything that exalts God causes the enemy to scatter.

**Ps 68:1**
*Let God arise, let his enemies be scattered: let them also that hate him flee before him.*

When we lift Him up, all men are drawn to Him. The key to effective warfare using Praise and Worship is focus and theme. Try to use songs that convey the message that is needed at the time. For example, if you are waging war on the enemy, songs that depicts the enemy's defeat and Christ's victory would be appropriate. Stay focused and remember that you are warring with a purpose and intent in mind.

The presence of God always manifests itself during true worship. In John 4:24, Jesus explained to the woman at the well that God was seeking those who worshipped in spirit and in truth. His statement makes us aware that there are those who have been or are worshipping in another way. The other way is called will worship. The **KEY** to true worship is in understanding the difference between it and will worship. Will worship is mentioned in Collossians.

## Will Worship:

**Colossians 2:23**
*Which things have indeed a shew of wisdom in <u>will worship</u>, and humility, and neglecting of the body; not in any honour to the satisfying of the flesh.*

The Greek word for will worship is 'ethelothreskeia' it is a voluntary, arbitrary worship which one prescribes and devises for himself, contrary to the contents and nature of faith which ought to be directed to Christ. It is also described as misdirected zeal. Note that will worship satisfies the flesh as it is focused on personal gratification than Christ glorification. I see many people come to church for will worship. They want the musician to excite them not lead them. How do I know? Because it is amazing that a musician can hit the chords of the organ and instantaneously one begins to dance. Once he stops, immediately one stops dancing. Others refuse to sing if their favorite song is not being sung. The organ is controlling the worship. Other times it is a program or what seems to be a good idea. It should be the Spirit of God who is in control.

Will worship also includes what I call prostitution worship. This is when our motives for worshipping are based on needs or wants we desire for God to instantly provide. We try to seduce him with our praise and expect a 'paycheck' of a blessing in return. Whenever you worship outside of the intent to make God feel good it becomes will worship because He is not the object of affection.

## True Worship

True worship is God centered. Its entire purpose is to entertain God, not the people nor ourselves. It is to satisfy God's need for adoration at whatever cost and expense. We cannot yield to the competitive spirit in the church that causes us to strive in the flesh. We have allowed the spirit of deception to reign rampant in our services. We seek the accolades of other ministers, churches and organizations and the act of worship in many instances have become a performance.

**John 4:23-4**
*But the hour cometh, and now is, when the true worshippers shall worship the Father in spirit and in truth: for the Father seeketh such to worship him. God is a Spirit: and they that worship him must worship him in spirit and in truth.*

Worship here is the Greek word proskuneo meaning to kiss, like a dog licking his master's hand, to crouch to prostrate oneself in homage, to kiss the hand to (toward) one, in token of reverence. In the New Testament by kneeling or prostration to do homage (to one) or make obeisance, whether in order to express respect or to make supplication; used to men and beings of superior rank.

The question is 'When last have you paid homage to God like this?' Praise, Worship and Warfare are a trinity that cannot be separated. True worship is humbling to your flesh. It is total abandon to God and total submission to His Spirit.

## ■ Children's Praise

Many times we underestimate the power of pure praise. When children praise the Lord whether in song or prayer, the enemy is silenced. The strength that comes forth from their mouths paralyzes the enemy. If he is silenced, he cannot communicate his destructive plans. Utilize children by first teaching them the significance of warfare, the Lordship of Christ and their authority as a believer. I recommend reading my training manual for children entitled God's Big Little Army.

**Ps 8:2**
*Out of the mouth of babes and sucklings hast thou ordained **strength (praise)** because of thine enemies, that thou mightest still the enemy and the avenger.*

'Strength' is the Hebrew word 'oz' which is also a word for praise. What a wonderful sound it must be to the ears of God to hear children praise Him!

## DISCERNMENT

Discernment is not a weapon it is a necessity in warfare. This is the ability to accurately determine between good and evil, right and wrong with consideration given to timing, atmosphere and mood. Many times you can determine which spirit or family of spirits is in operation. Devil spirits manifest themselves by creating actions relating to their area of ruling thereby revealing who they are. For example, if a person is extremely destructive in that it seems as if everything they touch or do is damaged in some way, the devil spirit named destruction is in operation.

In order to make this example clearer, let me share a personal experience. My mother was involved with such a destructive person. He was physically abusive, destroyed three cars within months, and constantly wreaked havoc everywhere he went. The spirit of destruction works with anger, death and violence. The spirit in this man attracted other people who hosted similar spirits. This involvement eventually caused her death – she died of multiple stab wounds. She died a violent death as a result of a violent, destructive spirit.

The warrior must make sure that he or she is not pledging allegiance with devil spirits through relationships. These unholy alliances defeat your effectiveness in warfare. Never side with the enemy, it will cloud your discernment. Being engaged in warfare demands that you are able to recognize the enemy you are fighting, the season you, your church or the people you are interceding for are in.

If you incorrectly discern, then you will employ the wrong strategy and your warfare will not be as effective as it could be. Discernment comes through, study of the Word, prayer and observation. If you study God who is the real thing, you will be able to determine the enemy who is the false thing.

> **Hebrews 5:14**
> *But strong meat belongeth to them that are of full age, even those who by reason of use have their senses exercised to discern both good and evil.*

> **Matt 16:3**
> *And in the morning, It will be foul weather to day: for the sky is red and lowring. O ye hypocrites, ye can discern the face of the sky; but can ye not discern the signs of the times?*

## IMAGINATION

This may sound 'New Age' but is not. You may have heard the notions 'Think it and you will have it'. Using your godly imagination in warfare assists you to 'see' the enemy in retreat and the impact of your weapons. In your mind's eye you determine what the outcome of your warfare. Based upon scriptures declaring we are overcomers, you are able to imagine victory. If you see it, you can have it. If you think it, you can possess it.

Your spiritual eyes enable you to see in the spirit realm. The Bible refers to imaginations of men that resulted in evil acts. If their evil imaginations produced wrongful deeds, what can a pure imagination accomplish? I am of the notion that you can have a pure imagination if you cast down all imaginations that exalt itself against the knowledge of Christ. In this sense, you utilize your imagination out of a pure heart to see an end to the enemy.

# 5

# PROPHETIC GESTURES

*The actions prove what the heart believes.*

Many people have mentioned using prophetic gestures but few have explained them. From personal experience and encounters with the demonic I know that prophetic gestures are real. The kingdom of darkness uses signs and gesticulations to cast curses, in incantations and summoning demonic help. We use prophetic gestures to impact the spirit world by praising God, deploying weapons and demolishing strongholds.

The scriptures declare that the Lord is the One who teaches our hands to war. Teach is the word lamad- in Psalm 144:1, that means to be trained for any hostile encounters. Our hands have to be taught and trained.

> **Ps 144:1**
> *Blessed be the LORD my strength, which*
> *teacheth my hands to war, and my fingers*
> *to fight:*

A prophetic gesture in its simplest term is a movement or position of the hand, arm, body, head or face to express an idea or emotion. This action is performed with the intent of forth telling or fore telling spiritual entities to obey a command that is gesticulated. The following are a list of the most commonly used actions in warfare.

## SHOUTING

Shouting means to cry out or call out in a loud voice.

> **Ps 78:65**
> *Then the Lord awaked as one out of sleep, and like a mighty man that shouteth by reason of wine.*

## SMITING

This is to injure or slay by hitting hard, to affect strongly and suddenly, to hit hard as if or with the hand.

> **Psalm 3:7**
> *Arise, O LORD and save me, Oh my God: for thou has smitten all mine enemies upon the cheekbone; thou has broken the teeth of the ungodly.*

> **Ps 78:66**
> *And he smote his enemies in the hinder parts: he put them to a perpetual reproach.*

> **Ezekiel 21:17**
> *I will also smite mine hands together, and I will cause my fury to rest: I the LORD have said it.*

## BREAKING

Breaking means to split into pieces, to smash, to crack or fracture, to make useless by smashing. It also means, to weaken the force of, to enter property by force, to train into obedience, to stop suddenly.

Having your fists closed as if holding something performs the prophetic gesture. With quick sharp moves, move your hands in an upward yet opposite position. Imagine breaking a pencil or chains of bondage. This is commonly used when declaring liberty over a person, city or situation.

**Ps 18:34**
*He teacheth my hands to war, so that a bow of steel is broken by mine arms.*

**Psalm 89:10**
*Thou hast broken Rahab in pieces, as one that is slain; thou hast scattered thine enemies with thy strong arm*

## CLAPPING

Clapping means to strike your hands together, more than once with palms facing each other.

There are different kinds of claps. There is an adoration clap given unto God in the form of an applause depicting our appreciation of Him.

Another type is the scattering clap. These are sharp quick claps as in scattering chickens. This is used to instruct demonic forces to break up and dismember themselves from each other therefore bringing division within their ranks.

Finally, there is a clap that brings order. This is rhythmic in nature it is slower than the applause and scattering claps and it decrees order as if you are marching to the tune of an army chant.

**Psalm 47:1**
*O clap your hands all ye people; shout unto God with the voice of triumph.*

**Psalm 68:1**
*Let God arise, let his enemies be scattered: let them also that hate him flee before him.*

## LAUGHING

Laughing expresses derision or mockery, to ridicule and find amusing. Laughing is used to emphasize the victory we have over the enemy. It is a disrespectful motion against the enemy further revealing his loss in battle and highlighting the shame thereof.

**Psalm 2:4**
*He that sitteth in the heavens shall laugh at them; thou shalt have all the heathen in derision.*

**Psalm 59:8**
*But thou, O LORD, shall laugh at them; thou shalt have all the heathen in derision.*

## TREADING

Treading means to trample underfoot by walking or dancing. This is used to express and exercise dominion and authority of evil forces in operation. You will see this treading motion through many tribal dances in African and Indian cultures. In the days of old, treading was used in the winepress. People would tread on the grapes to crush and squeeze the juices out of them.

**Psalm 44:5 & 12**
*Through thee will we push down our enemies: through thy name will we tread them under that rise up against us. Through our God we shall do valiantly; for he it is that shall tread down our enemies.*

**Luke 10:19**
*Behold, I give unto you power to tread on
serpents and scorpions, and over all the power
of the enemy; and nothing shall by any means
hurt you.*

**Zechariah 10:5**
*And they shall be as mighty men, which tread
down their enemies in the mire of the streets in
the battle: and they shall fight, because the
LORD is with them, and the riders in horses
shall be confounded.*

# PUSHING

This is the act of pressing against a thing with enough force to
move it, to exert a thrusting force upon something. It denotes
resistance to the enemy's attack and the forcing into retreat his
devil spirits.

**Psalm 44:5**
*Through thee we will push down our enemies:
through thy name will we tread them under
that rise up against us.*

# POINTING

This indicates position or direction using an outstretched index
finger. It is used to assert one's authority over a lesser ranking
individual as well as instructing or commanding that spirit to
perform a desired action such as departing.

**Luke 11:20**
*But if I with the finger of God cast out devils, no
doubt the kingdom of God is come upon you.*

## PIERCING

This means to force a way into or through something, to make a hole. Piercing in warfare is done with the hand as if holding a sword and thrusting forward. Remember the Word of God is the Sword of the Spirit, piercing between spirit and soul.

> **Leviticus 26:7**
> *And ye shall chase your enemies, ad they shall fall before you by the sword.*

> **Hebrews 4:12**
> *For the word of God is quick, and powerful, and sharper than any two-edged sword, piercing even to the dividing asunder of soul and spirit, and of the joints and marrow, and is a discerner of the thoughts and intents of the heart.*

## SHOOTING ARROWS

This gesture is performed with the hands as if using a bow and arrow. The intent is to divide the enemy and cause them to scatter.

> **Psalm 18:4**
> *Yea, he sent out his arrows, and scattered them; and he shot out lightnings, and discomfited them.*

## SHAKING

This means to cause a thing to be forced off by sharp quick movements, to tremble. Imagine shaking a dirty rug and repeat that action in warfare. It is used to remove anything not of God that is trying to cling to a person or city.

**Zechariah 2:9**
*For, behold, I will shake mine hand upon them,
and they shall be spoil to their servants: and ye
shall know that the LORD of hosts hath sent me.*

**Isaiah 52:2**
*Shake thyself from the dust; arise, and sit
down, O Jerusalem: loose thyself from the
bands of thy neck, O captive daughter of Zion.*

# BINDING

To bind means to fasten or circle with a cord, to secure in place
to constrain by oath or law. Using the hands imagine binding
a bundle of sticks together. This symbolizes powerlessness on
the enemy's part. This is especially useful in deliverance. I often
command a person to sit in a chair and with this prophetic gesture bind them in that chair. This prevents them from lunging
forward at you and from any sudden movements. I believe that
when the gesture is executed, an angel of God is restricting and
carrying out that command in the spirit.

**Psalm 149:8**
*To bind their kings with chains, and their
nobles with fetters of iron;*

A final note on prophetic gestures. They are just gestures. These
are not to be taken as a course of physical action to be inflicted
on another physical person. These gestures have spiritual significance only and should not be used in natural situations.

Bear in mind that these are used against the enemy in spiritual
warfare. These actions in and of themselves are useless without
the Word of God and the Spirit of God. The Word of God must
be used and the leading of His Spirit must be followed.

# NOTES

CHAPTER

# 6

# PRAISE & WORSHIP

*"When we believe that we should be satisfied rather than God glorified in our worship, then we put God below ourselves as though He had been made for us rather than we had been made for him."*

*Stephen Charnock*

Praise and worship in its broadest definition is, the act of rendering homage to God in forms of celebration and acts of service. It is the expression of admiration, great respect and gratitude to a superior being.

Praise means to glorify, commend highly, magnify and exalt God. Too often, we glorify ourselves by giving a party to our flesh. This is seen when worship services become choir competitions and conferences become exhibitions. I say this because often times when someone is leading a song, I will hear the audience say ' Sing girl, boy that girl can sing.' We end up praising and congratulating the singer but not the Lord. This must change for effective warfare. You have to have a personal praise and worship relationship with the Lord. He has to receive true praise and worship from your spirit (John 4:24), the innermost part of your core being, not your excited flesh.

Below are the Biblical definitions of praise. I challenge you to physically perform each of these privately and publicly. Doing these actions bring about a humility and a liberation from what others think about you. Humility always brings promotion from the Lord.

The Bible has a lot to say about praise and worship. The biblical definitions are always the most accurate. Explore with me the wonders of praise.

**Yadah:** To use your hands physically, to extend hands in reverence or worship, to give thanks.

> **Psalm 9:1**
> *I will **praise** you, O Lord, with my whole heart;*
> *I will tell of your marvelous works.*

**Zamar:** To use fingers to play musical instruments accompanied with voice, to celebrate in song and music, to sing forth praises.

> **Psalm 21:13**
> *Be exalted, O Lord, in your own strength! We*
> *will sing and praise your power.*

**Halal:** To make a show, to boast and thus act clamorously foolish, to rave, celebrate.

> **1 Chronicles 23:30**
> *..stand every morning to thank and praise the*
> *Lord, and likewise at evening.*

**Shabach:** To address in a loud tone, to praise, to be loud, to adore.

> **Psalm 66:2**
> *Sing out he honor of His name; Make His*
> *praise glorious.*

**Tehillah:** To celebrate, laudation, song of praise.

> **Deuteronomy 26:19**
> *And to make thee high above all nations which*
> *he hath made, in praise, and in name, and in*

*honour; and that thou mayest be an holy people
unto the LORD thy God, as he hath spoken.*

**Todah:** A choir of worshippers, confession, praise.

### Psalm 42:4
*When I remember these things, I pour out my
soul in me: for I had gone with the multitude,
I went with them to the house of God, with the
voice of joy and praise, with a multitude that
kept holyday.*

When we praise, the Lord inhabits, comes and lives in the midst of our request or situation. He delights in our praise. Notice that praise is a LOUD thing, an OBVIOUS thing, an EXPRESSIVE thing. 'Well, I will just praise God in my heart', I have heard people say – well, praise originates in your heart but is expressed through your PHYSICAL participation. If you are not exercising your praise in one of the above listed biblical definitions I am concerned about you. If you are not able to be bold in your personal worship of Christ how will you declare authority over attacking spirits? No, if you are not expressing praise, you are just thinking about it. Thinking about it is futile as faith without works (proof of belief) is dead.

The Israelites used singers in battle. They understood the importance of exalting God. Look at the result of praising. When praise is optimum it will be hard for anything else to happen – the ministers could not even preach! How wonderful it is to praise God for all he has done.

### 2 Chronicles 5:13-14
*It came even to pass, as the trumpeters and
singers were as one, to make one sound to be*

*heard in praising and thanking the LORD;*
*and when they lifted up their voice with the*
*trumpets and cymbals and instruments of*
*musick, and praised the LORD, saying, For he*
*is good; for his mercy endureth for ever: that*
*then the house was filled with a cloud, even the*
*house of the LORD; So that the priests could not*
*stand to minister by reason of the cloud: for the*
*glory of the LORD had filled the house of God.*

## WORSHIP

We worship the Lord because he commanded us to (Deuteronomy 6:13). Worship is an expression of our love for God. It is evidence that we are thankful for what he has done, but most importantly that we love Him for who He is. Friend, Redeemer, Father. Comforter, He is all these and more.

**Shachah:** To fall down prostrate before the Lord, to pay homage to royalty, to fall down flat.

### 1 Chronicles 16:29
*Give unto the LORD the glory due unto his*
*name: bring an offering, and come before him:*
*worship the LORD in the beauty of holiness.*

**Proskuneo:** To adore, to kiss the hand to (toward) one, in token of reverence among the Orientals, especially the Persians, to fall upon the knees and touch the ground with the forehead as an expression of profound reverence, to kiss like a dog licking his master's hand.

### Matthew 2:8
*And he sent them to Bethlehem, and said, Go*
*and search diligently for the young child; and*
*when ye have found him, bring me word again.*

**Sebomai:** To be devout in religious service

> **Acts 18:13**
> *Saying, This fellow persuadeth men to worship*
> *God contrary to the law.*

True praise and worship always originates out of the spirit. It is not ashamed it bold and confident.

## PROPHETIC SONG & PROPHETIC PRAISE

Prophetic song and or prophetic praise in their broadest terms are the praising or singing that is directed by the Holy Spirit. Prophetic song is equivalent to the Lord's Song or a New Song. This is when you declare new things from the heart of God to the city, people, nation or situation. It is not difficult at all. Try this exercise:

Choose the melody of a song that you enjoy. I chose 'There Is None Like You'. Begin by singing that melody with the correct words, then create your own words that line up with God's Word. So, instead of your song sounding like:

> *There is none like you*
> *No one else can touch my heart like you do*
> *I could search throughout eternity Lord*
> *And find, there is none like you.*

It may prophetically become:

> *You are worthy Lord*
> *All the nations must bow down before you*
> *Every spirit must yield to your Word*
> *For you are Lord over all.*

You can also sing the rhythm in tongues. As you become more comfortable, you can branch off into new melodies and words fresh from the throne of God. You do not have to have a singing voice. You just need boldness and obedience to The Voice of the Spirit. If you are in a corporate service and are singing in tongues loud enough to prophesy you must interpret that which was sung or it was only for your benefit. This statement is made under the impression that you were prophesying according to the order and flow of that local assembly. During your own personal worship, nothing hinders you from singing in the Spirit and singing new songs to the Lord.

Prophetic praise is similar to prophetic song except it involves instruments. The drums, piped instruments, tambourines etc. are all able to participate in prophetic praise. This is when there is an unprecedented melody or tune flowing from these instruments with the sole purpose of exalting God or destroying the enemy.

In a lot of foreign countries, music is used to perform incantations of evil spirits. The spirit world is aware of the dangerous impact of perfected and prophetic praise.

I am from a musical family and a Caribbean country. Music has the ability to create moods, feelings, sensations and responses. For example, you can hear a song on the radio that used to be 'your song' and immediately your mind travels back in time. If permitted to go further, you will remember where you were, what you were doing, with whom and your body will begin dancing!

Music is a POWERFUL tool. Used correctly and under the inspiration of the Spirit of God, it can wreak havoc on the enemy. It also, creates atmospheres for God to manifest Himself.

# 7

# PRAYER – A VITAL TOOL

*"A man is powerful on his knees."*

*Corrie Ten Boon*

The Bible shows the absolute necessity of prayer.

### II Chronicles 7:14
*"If my people who are called by my name, will humble themselves and pray and seek my face and turn from their wicked ways, then will I hear from heaven and will forgive their sin and will heal their land."*

## WHY SHOULD BELIEVERS PRAY?

■ **God's house is called a house of prayer.**

### Isaiah 56:7
*'..for mine house shall be called an house of prayer...'*

■ **God's word says that we are to pray without ceasing.**

### Ephesians 6:18
*'Praying always with all prayer and supplication in the Spirit...'*

■ **All men everywhere are to pray.**

### I Timothy 2:8
*'I will therefore that men pray everywhere, lifting up holy hands...'*

- ## We are disciples of Christ and He prayed.

  **Mark 1:35**
  *'...Jesus got up, left the house and went off to a solitary place, where he prayed.'*

## WHAT IS PRAYER?

Prayer is the means by which we express our love, adoration, needs and desires to God. It is the tool by which we become intimate with God. It is spending time in conversation with God. It is talking to God as you would talk to a friend.

## How Should We Pray?

- *We should pray in faith believing that God will do what He says.*

- *We should pray without wavering.* ***Mark 11:24***

- *We should pray according to God's will.* ***I John 5:14-16***

- *We should pray God's word because it does not return to Him void.* ***Isaiah 55:11***

- *We should pray in Jesus' name.* ***John 14:14***

- *'If you ask anything in my name, I will do it.'*

- *In agreement. If you are praying individually, pray in agreement with   God's word. If more than one person is praying, agree with them and God's word.*

- *We should pray in the Spirit.* ***Romans 8:26-27***

- *We should pray in tongues* ***I Corinthians 14:14***

## WHAT HINDERS OUR PRAYERS?

■ **Not giving honor to your wife.**
**I Peter 3:7**
*'Likewise ye husbands, dwell with them according to knowledge, giving honour unto the wife, as unto the weaker vessel, and as being heirs together of the grace of life; that your prayers be not hindered.'*

■ **Impure Motives.**
**James 4:3**
*'Ye ask, and receive not, because you ask amiss, that you may consume it upon your lusts.'*

■ **Iniquity/ Sin/ Wrong doing.**
**Isaiah 59:2**
*'But your iniquities have separated between you and your God, and your sins have hid His face from you, that He will not hear.'*

■ **Unforgiveness.**
**Mark 11:26**
*'but if ye do not forgive, neither will your Father which is in heaven forgive your trespasses.'*

■ **Doubt.**
**James 1:6-7**
*'But let him ask in faith nothing wavering. For he that waivereth is like a wave of the sea driven with the wind and tossed. For let not that man think that he shall receive anything of the Lord.'*

■ **Stinginess.**
**Proverbs 21:13**
*'Whoso stoppeth his ear at the cry of the poor, he also shall cry himself, but shall not be heard.'*

## DEFINITIONS OF PRAYER:

The following examples will show you that prayer is a **VERBAL** thing. You cannot be meditating or thinking in your mind and call that prayer. Prayer is active and powerful. I listed the Hebrew and Greek words so that a graphic picture of prayer would be displayed.

## Old Testament Hebrew Definitions:

i. **PALAI** as used in Genesis 20:7 which make supplication, entreat, intercede.

ii. **ATHAR** is used in Job 33:26 means to listen.

iii. **SIYACH** used in Psalm 55:17 this means to converse aloud, talk with, commune, speak, complain or declare.

iv. **CHALAH** as used in Zechariah 7:2 is like a woman in travail.

## New Testament Greek Definitions:

i. **DEOMAI** is used in Matthew 9:38. This means to make a request, beseech, beg or petition.

ii. **PROSEUCHOMAI** is used in Matthew 26:36. This means to earnestly call near or to invite.

iii. **PARAKALEO** used in Matthew 26:53. This means to call for or invoke

iv. **EUCHOMAI** is used in II Corinthians 13:7. This means to pray to God or to wish.

## TYPES OF PRAYER

A. **Praise Sample Statement:** *You are worthy Lord, you are awesome, beautiful, magnificent and glorious.*

B. **Thanksgiving**- This is my response to the goodness and graciousness of God. Thanksgiving is thanking God for what He has done and what He is going to do. It is being grateful for all He has done.

   **Sample Statement:** *Thank you Lord, for my children, my job and my home. I appreciate your goodness towards me.*

   > **Psalm 51:1**
   > *'What shall I render to the Lord for all His benefits toward me? "To thee I shall offer a sacrifice of thanksgiving."'*

C. **Confession** – Confession is agreeing with God about your sin: it is your response to His holiness and the verbal acknowledgement that you have not kept His standards.

   **Sample Statement:** *Father, I confess that I committed for-nication etc.*

   > **Psalm 66:18**
   > *'If I regard wickedness in my heart, the Lord will not hear.'*

D. **Intercession** – This is when you go to God on behalf of another person. Below a⸍ mands. We are to pray for:

   *All saints, family, friends etc. - Ephe*

*All men & political authorities -* **Timothy 2:1**

*Those who labor in the gospel, 5-fold, ministers etc. -* **Ephesians6:19,20,**

*Those in adversity & each another -* **Hebrews 13:3 ,James 5:16**

*For the sending of Laborers -* **Matthew 9:38**

We need to remember to pray for the heads of governments in the world especially our President. The Bible shows us that we need to pray for them so we can live a peaceable life.

**Sample Statement:** *Father, I come on the behalf of my pastor and I am asking that you meet his financial needs.*

E.  **Petition** – Petition is asking God for needs and concerns that pertain to you. It is your response to the power and wisdom of God as your Heavenly Father. As children, we do not hesitate to tell our parents what we need or desire. We need to ask God with the same kind of child-like faith.

> **John 15:7**
> *If you abide in me and my word abide in you,*
> *ask whatever you wish and it shall be done*
> *for you.*

**Sample Statement:** *Lord, I know you are My healer. I am asking you to heal me of this illness.*

**rfare** – This is your response to God's might. It is taking ʷeapons of God according to Ephesians 6:12-19 and demanding the Devil to stop interfering in your life or the lives of others.

**Sample Statement:** *Satan, you have no authority in my finances, I command you to cease your attack in Jesus' name.*

G. **Supplication** – This is your response to God's mercy and grace. It is entreating and imploring God as in the case of being acquitted.

**Sample Statement:** *Father, forgive me for my sins.*

# NOTES

# TRADITIONAL MISTAKES

*"Ignorance is the mother of all mistakes."*

Some of the mistakes that we make in warfare though innocent are nevertheless mistakes that should be avoided.

- ❀ Sending the devil to hell. He is not going there until Jehovah sends him at the White Throne judgement (Revelation 20).

- ❀ Speaking to God instead of the enemy. In warfare, you address the enemy directly. Do not say ' Father I thank you that poverty is gone away.' Rather, say 'Poverty go in Jesus' name'.

- ❀ Misquoting scriptures or making them up.

- ❀ Confusion. Praying another prayer while the person who is leading corporate warfare is praying.

- ❀ Losing focus and praying for everything else, going off on a tangent. Stick with the subject. You cannot hit a bulls-eye if your darts are thrown off the board.

- ❀ Believing that emotional reactions result in spiritual intervention. God is move by faith, not by emotions.

# NOTES

CHAPTER

# 9

# WARFARE STRATEGY

*"There is no higher and simpler law of strategy than that of keeping one's forces concentrated."*

*Clausewitz*

There are several principles that were used to govern "war" in the Old Testament. Unjust violence was prohibited, but "war" as a part of ancient life was led (Judges 4:13). If war was preceded by sacrifices recognizing Gods' leadership and sovereignty as in 1 Samuel 7:9. Or if God was consulted and Israel obeyed, divine protection was promised (Deuteronomy 20:1-4). God's presence in battle was important and symbolized by the ark of the covenant (1 Sam. 4:3-11).

Before and during "battle," the Israelites used praise in the form of trumpets that were blown placing the cause before God in anticipation of the victory and gratitude for it (Num. 10:9-10), as well as to relay the orders of the commanders. The shofar or ram's horn was also used to call an assembly prior to war or prayer.

## CHARACTERISTICS OF WAR

❀ Those who were fearful were exempt (Deuteronomy. 20:5-8). God did not allow them into battle so that their fear would not permeate the camp.

❀ War was mainly conducted in the Spring of the year (2 Samuel 11:1).

✿ War tactics included surprize, ambush, pretended flight and surrounding the enemy (Genesis 14:15; Joshua 8:2-7; 2 Samuel 5:23).

✿ Warfare was planned. They prepared for war by cutting off their enemies water supply and setting the city on fire (Judges 9:52).

✿ People who were ill and pregnant women did not attend war. Women in general and children did not engage in warfare. In spiritual warfare however, there is no gender. The age of men were between 20 –50 years of age.

## SAMPLE WARFARE PRAYER STRATEGY

If you are hosting an all night prayer meeting with the intent to intercept and defeat enemy activity, or if you are planning an all night praise and prayer meeting, you could use these sample strategies.

| **A War Cry – A Call to the Occasion (Joshua 6:5)** |
| --- |
| Some people use a trumpet, a shout or a shofar in rallying the people for prayer. |
| **Praise & Worship 30-60 minutes** |
| Incorporate instruments, singing, dancing, flags etc. |

*Always begin with a Call to Prayer and Praise & Worship. Utilize one of the three strategies listed below or create your own.*

| Strategy A | Strategy B | Strategy C |
| --- | --- | --- |
| Pray over topic or against evil spirit until breakthrough. Praise songs or music celebrating victory. Repeat this pattern until the meeting ends. End the time of prayer with praise. | Rotate prayers between intercession, warfare and praise. Utilize children to pray for other children or issues relevant to them. | Prayers of thanksgiving and use of positive declarations mixed with praise, dance, flags, banners etc. Thanking God for peace, resolve, victory etc. |

The sample can be modified with the amount of spirits you are dealing with. One of my favorite warfare strategies is praising just as passionately as you fight. In other words, every time you attack the enemy, praise the Lord with as much energy. I call this the **rest and war strategy**. The praise and worship though directed toward God, renews you. In His presence is fullness of joy and Zechariah says that the joy of the Lord is our strength.

Another time you may do a **Jericho march**. This is when you march around a building or area silently, the praisers and priests in front and then you shout loudly on the seventh march. God may instruct you to **use banners, tambourines and dance** at another time. You also could cut out pictures of countries with the faces of people from those countries and place them on **poster boards**. These become visual objects of focus during prayer. Whatever the method, utilize the art of strategy.

Another strategy is praying the news or headlines. Cut out the headlines or articles from the newspaper and pray over them. On Mondays you may pray over national political issues. On Tuesdays, medical research and so forth. God can use you to change the headlines.

**OBEDIENCE** is the key to any victory. Ask the Lord for a strategy. When the Israelites fought their enemies, they listened to the Lord to see if they should fight, how should they fight and would they win. The battle at Ai was different from the one at Jericho and the one Gideon fought against the Midianites. Revelation knowledge is important. Rely on and trust in the Lord for your strategy and victory.

# NOTES

# CHAPTER
# 10

# THINGS YOU SHOULD KNOW

*Minds are like parachutes, they only function when open.*

## OFFENSIVE & DIRECTIONAL COMMUNICATION

When speaking to the enemy in warfare avoid statements such as:

*Lord, please let the devil leave me alone.*

*Father, I need you to fight this devil.*

*Dear Lord the spirit is attacking us so now loose him.*

These are statements of supplication and not war. They are defensive rather than offensive. In warfare, remember you have a goal and an aim. That goal is to annihilate the enemy's attacks and destroy his works. Speak directly to the spirit and command him or her to go, flee, be bound etc. For example, instead you might say:

*Poverty, in the name of Jesus I arrest you and command you to loose the finances of the people. I declare that your works are of no effect and the Lord rebuke you now.*

## DECLARATIONS

This is an announcement. You are telling the spirit world what will happen. Under the authority of Christ, you tell evil forces what is happening. You are declaring, pronouncing and announcing to the world that which God has said in His word. For example you might say:

*I declare that wealth and riches are in my house, poverty has no authority here. According to the word in Deuteronomy 8:18, I have the ability to create wealth and that ability is in effect now.*

## WARFARE VERBAGE:

| DON"T'S (to the enemy) | DO'S (In Jesus' Name) |
|---|---|
| Please | I command you |
| Thank you | I bind you, loose your hold |
| Have mercy | I arrest you, You must |
| Why don't you leave me alone? | The Lord rebuke you, I forbid you to… |
| Can you go now? | Leave now, back up, |
| Give me a break, I have a lot going on right now. | I neutralize your power, I overturn your wisdom tables |

## THINGS TO ALWAYS DO

After engaging in spiritual warfare on any level, it is imperative that you **cancel the assignment of Revenge & Retaliation**. These two spirits are unleashed to wreaked havoc as a counter attack. Cancel their plans before they complete them!

### COMMON DEVIL SPIRITS
### FOUGHT ON A PERSONAL LEVEL

| NAME | ACTIVITY / DESCRIPTION |
|---|---|
| Anger | Fury, hatred, spite, animosity |
| Barrenness | Fruitless, impotence, unproductive |
| Bitterness | Resentment, unforgiveness, gall |
| Control | Witchcraft, Jezebel, possession |
| Fear | Of failure, rejection, sickness |
| Guilt | Condemnation, shame, |
| Inferiority | Low self esteem, self – hatred |
| Rebellion | Self-will, selfishness, pride, hatred of authority |
| Despair | Depression, discouragement |
| Doubt | Unbelief, skepticism |
| Jealousy | Envy, suspicion |
| Perversity | Avarice, lust, fornication, pornography, adultery, molestation, perversion, sexual impurity, covetousness |
| Pride | Stubbornness, power, position |
| Religion | Doctrinal obsession, legalism |

# REFERENCES

**Mysterious Secrets Of the Dark Kingdom**
- The Battle For Planet Earth – J.P. Timmons

The Demon Hit List
- Apostle John Eckhard *Crusaders Ministries*

**Vine's Expository Dictionary**
- W.E. Vine

**Strong's Exhaustive Concordance**

**Brown Driver Briggs Hebrew & English Lexicon**
- Brown-Driver-Briggs

# OTHER MATERIALS BY SARA M. CONNER

**God's Big Little Army...$8.00**
This book is simple and straightforward. It was used as a curriculum in South Africa to train children workers as they equipped children in spritual warfare. Children will learn how to speak in tongues among other things.

**Success Sayings For Singles...$10.00**
A collection of delightful quotes which, encourage and inspire singles to live a life of purity and purpose.

**My Mother Myself...$7.00**
An interesting audio message on the influence of the first woman in your life. If your relationship with your mother was a little less than perfect, then you need this tape!

**In The Storm...$7.00**
Have you wondered why it seems you are in a continual storm? A cycle of bad events? Would you like to get out of the storm? Learn the number one key to changing your current situation!

**Believe & Receive...$7.00**
Learn the exciting way to really receive what God has for you. This time proven method has helped hundreds of people receive their God given blessings. Spoken by Eben Conner. Get it today!

### Contact Information:

If you would like a product mailed to you
or if you would like to contact Eben or Sara Conner,

please email us at:
admin@wotfc.com
Or call: (817) 453-8222

# NOTES

# NOTES

# NOTES

Made in the USA
Columbia, SC
15 January 2020